Benedetto
MARCELLO

(1686 – 1739)

Sonata for Treble (Alto) Recorder and Basso continuo, Op. 2
F Major / Fa majeur / F-Dur

Edited by
Manfredo Zimmermann

DOWANI International

Preface

This Sonata in F Major for treble (alto) recorder and basso continuo Op. 2, by Benedetto Marcello, has been edited and recorded by Manfredo Zimmermann, professor of recorder at the Wuppertal Musikhochschule and a specialist in early music. As with Marcello's D minor Sonata, which has already appeared in a DOWANI edition, this piece is noteworthy for its highly idiomatic writing for the recorder; the music seems to lie perfectly under the fingers.

The CD opens with the concert version of each movement. After tuning your instrument (Track 1), the musical work can begin. Your first practice session should be in the slow tempo. If your stereo system is equipped with a balance control, you can, by turning the control, smoothly blend either the recorder or the harpsichord accompaniment into the foreground. The recorder, however, will always remains audible – even if very quietly – as a guide. In the middle position, both instruments can be heard at the same volume. If you do not have a balance control, you can listen to the solo instrument on one loudspeaker and to the harpsichord on the other. Having mastered the piece at slow tempo, you can practice the second and fourth movements at medium tempo. We have omitted the medium tempo for the first and third movements, which are already relatively slow in the original. Now you can play the piece with accompaniment at the original tempo. At the medium and original tempos, the continuo accompaniment can be heard on both channels (without recorder) in stereo quality. All of the versions were recorded live. The names of the musicians are listed on the last page of this volume; further information can be found in the Internet at www.dowani.com.

In keeping with their style, the slow movements of this piece rely heavily on elements of improvisation. We have therefore included only the most essential embellishments and phrase marks. Players are invited to add trills, mordents, slurs and so forth at their own discretion. The same holds true, of course, for the realization of the figured bass (basso continuo or harpsichord), as can clearly be heard on the recording.

We wish you lots of fun playing from our DOWANI 3 Tempi Play Along editions and hope that your musicality and diligence will enable you to play the concert version as soon as possible. Our goal is to provide the essential conditions you need for effective practicing through motivation, enjoyment and fun.

Your DOWANI Team

Avant-propos

Manfredo Zimmermann, professeur de flûte à bec au Conservatoire Supérieur de Wuppertal et spécialiste dans le domaine de la musique ancienne, a édité et enregistré la présente sonate pour flûte à bec alto et basse continue op. 2 en Fa majeur de Benedetto Marcello. Tout comme la sonate en ré mineur qui est déjà parue aux Editions DOWANI, cette œuvre présente l'écriture typique de la flûte à bec ; par conséquent son exécution ne pose pas de problèmes techniques majeurs.

Le CD vous permettra d'entendre d'abord la version de concert de chaque mouvement. Après avoir accordé votre instrument (plage n° 1), vous pourrez commencer le travail musical. Le premier contact avec le morceau devrait se faire à un tempo lent. Si votre chaîne hi-fi dispose d'un réglage de balance, vous pouvez l'utiliser pour mettre au premier plan soit la flûte à bec, soit l'accompagnement au clavecin. La flûte à bec restera cependant toujours audible très doucement à l'arrière-plan. En équilibrant la balance, vous entendrez les deux instruments à volume égal. Si vous ne disposez pas de réglage de balance, vous entendrez l'instrument soliste sur un des haut-parleurs et le clavecin sur l'autre. Après avoir étudié le morceau à un tempo lent, vous pourrez ensuite travailler le 2ème et le 4ème mouvement à un tempo modéré (seulement avec l'accompagnement de la basse continue). Le 1er et le 3ème mouvement ne sont pas proposés dans un tempo modéré, car leurs tempos originaux sont déjà relativement lents. Vous pourrez ensuite jouer le tempo original. Dans ces deux tempos vous entendrez l'accompagnement de la basse continue sur les deux canaux en stéréo (sans la partie de flûte à bec). Toutes les versions ont été enregistrées en direct. Vous trouverez les noms des artistes qui ont participé aux enregistrements sur la dernière page de cette édition ; pour obtenir plus de renseignements, veuillez consulter notre site Internet : www.dowani.com.

Suivant le style de l'époque, les mouvements lents de cette œuvre laissent beaucoup de place à l'improvisation ; c'est pourquoi nous n'avons noté que très peu d'ornements et de phrasés. Chaque musicien peut ou doit ajouter ses propres indications (trilles, mordants, liaisons etc.). Cela concerne également la réalisation de la basse chiffrée (basse continue ou clavecin) – comme on l'entend bien sur notre enregistrement.

Nous vous souhaitons beaucoup de plaisir à faire de la musique avec la collection *DOWANI 3 Tempi Play Along* et nous espérons que votre musicalité et votre application vous amèneront aussi rapidement que possible à la version de concert. Notre but est de vous offrir les bases nécessaires pour un travail efficace par la motivation et le plaisir.

Les Éditions DOWANI

Vorwort

Manfredo Zimmermann, Professor für Blockflöte an der Musikhochschule Wuppertal und Spezialist für Alte Musik, hat die vorliegende Sonate für Altblockflöte und Basso continuo op. 2 in F-Dur von Benedetto Marcello herausgegeben und eingespielt. Wie auch die bereits bei DOWANI erschienene Sonate in d-moll zeichnet sich dieses Werk durch eine sehr blockflötistische Idiomatik aus; die Sonate liegt einfach hervorragend für dieses Instrument.

Auf der CD können Sie zuerst die Konzertversion eines jeden Satzes anhören. Nach dem Stimmen Ihres Instrumentes (Track 1) kann die musikalische Arbeit beginnen. Ihr erster Übe-Kontakt mit dem Stück sollte im langsamen Tempo stattfinden. Wenn Ihre Stereoanlage über einen Balance-Regler verfügt, können Sie durch Drehen des Reglers entweder die Blockflöte oder die Cembalobegleitung stufenlos in den Vordergrund blenden. Die Blockflöte bleibt jedoch immer – wenn auch sehr leise – hörbar. In der Mittelposition erklingen beide Instrumente gleich laut. Falls Sie keinen Balance-Regler haben, hören Sie das Soloinstrument auf dem einen Lautsprecher, das Cembalo auf dem anderen. Nachdem Sie das Stück im langsamen Tempo einstudiert haben, können Sie den zweiten und vierten Satz auch im mittleren Tempo üben. Beim ersten und dritten Satz haben wir auf das mittlere Tempo verzichtet, da sie im Original schon relativ langsam sind. Anschließend können Sie sich im Originaltempo begleiten lassen. Die Basso continuo-Begleitung erklingt im mittleren und originalen Tempo auf beiden Kanälen (ohne Blockflöte) in Stereo-Qualität. Alle eingespielten Versionen wurden live aufgenommen. Die Namen der Künstler finden Sie auf der letzten Seite dieser Ausgabe; ausführlichere Informationen können Sie im Internet unter www.dowani.com nachlesen.

Da die langsamen Sätze dieses Werkes dem Stil entsprechend sehr stark auf improvisatorischen Elementen beruhen, wurden nur die nötigsten Verzierungen und Phrasierungen notiert. Der Spieler oder die Spielerin darf/soll gerne eigene Ergänzungen (Triller, Mordente, Bindungen usw.) hinzufügen. Dies gilt natürlich auch für die Ausführung des Generalbasses (Basso continuo oder Cembalo) – wie in der Aufnahme deutlich zu hören ist.

Wir wünschen Ihnen viel Spaß beim Musizieren mit unseren *DOWANI 3 Tempi Play Along*-Ausgaben und hoffen, dass Ihre Musikalität und Ihr Fleiß Sie möglichst bald bis zur Konzertversion führen werden. Unser Ziel ist es, Ihnen durch Motivation, Freude und Spaß die notwendigen Voraussetzungen für effektives Üben zu schaffen.

Ihr DOWANI Team

Sonata

for Treble (Alto) Recorder and Basso continuo, Op. 2
F Major / Fa majeur / F-Dur

B. Marcello (1686 – 1739)
Continuo Realization: M. Zimmermann

DOW 2509

Benedetto
MARCELLO

(1686 – 1739)

Sonata for Treble (Alto) Recorder and Basso continuo, Op. 2
F Major / Fa majeur / F-Dur

Treble (Alto) Recorder / Flûte à bec alto / Altblockflöte

DOWANI International

Recorder

Sonata

for Treble (Alto) Recorder and Basso continuo, Op. 2
F Major / Fa majeur / F-Dur

I ②

B. Marcello (1686 – 1739)

DOW 2509

3

III ④ Largo

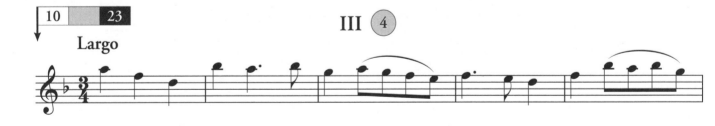

DOW 2509

4

Benedetto
MARCELLO

(1686 – 1739)

Sonata for Treble (Alto) Recorder and Basso continuo, Op. 2
F Major / Fa majeur / F-Dur

Basso continuo / Basse continue / Generalbass

DOWANI International

Basso continuo

Sonata

for Treble (Alto) Recorder and Basso continuo, Op. 2

F Major / Fa majeur / F-Dur

I

B. Marcello (1686 – 1739)

II

DOW 2509

III

4

IV

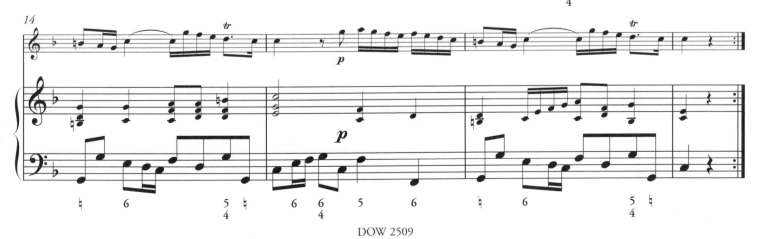

8

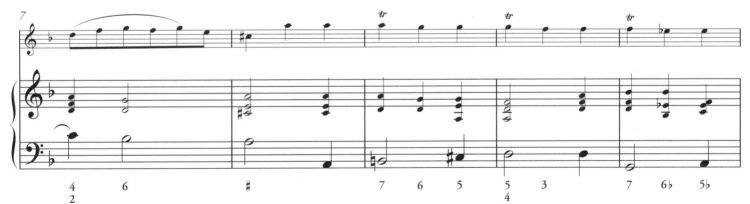

10

DOWANI CD:
- Track No. 1
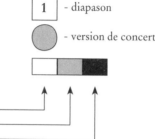
- tuning notes
- Track numbers in circles
- concert version
- Track numbers in squares

- slow Play Along Tempo
- intermediate Play Along Tempo
- original Play Along Tempo

- Additional tracks for longer movements or pieces
- **Concert version:** recorder and basso continuo
- **Slow tempo:** The recorder can be faded in or out by means of the balance control. Channel 1: recorder solo; channel 2: harpsichord accompaniment wit recorder in the background; middle position: both channels at the same volum
- **Intermediate tempo:** basso continuo only
- **Original tempo:** basso continuo only

DOWANI CD :
- Plage N° 1
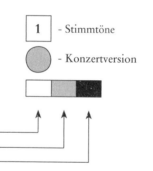
- diapason
- N° de plage dans un cercle
- version de concert
- N° de plage dans un rectangle

- tempo lent play along
- tempo moyen play along
- tempo original play along

- Plages supplémentaires pour mouvements ou morceaux longs
- **Version de concert :** flûte à bec et basse continue
- **Tempo lent :** Vous pouvez choisir – en réglant la balance du lecteur CD – entre les versions avec ou sans flûte à bec. 1ᵉʳ canal : flûte à bec solo ; 2ⁿᵈ canal : accompagnement de clavecin avec flûte à bec en fond sonore ; au milieu : les deux canaux au même volume
- **Tempo moyen :** seulement l'accompagnement de la basse continue
- **Tempo original :** seulement l'accompagnement de la basse continue

DOWANI CD:
- Track Nr. 1
- Stimmtöne
- Trackangabe im Kreis
- Konzertversion
- Trackangabe im Rechteck

- langsames Play Along Tempo
- mittleres Play Along Tempo
- originales Play Along Tempo

- Zusätzliche Tracks bei längeren Sätzen oder Stücken
- **Konzertversion:** Blockflöte und Basso continuo
- **Langsames Tempo:** Blockflöte kann mittels Balance-Regler ein- und ausgeblendet werden. 1. Kanal: Blockflöte solo; 2. Kanal: Cembalobegleitung mit Blockflöte im Hintergrund; Mitte: beide Kanäle in gleicher Lautstärke
- **Mittleres Tempo:** nur Basso continuo
- **Originaltempo:** nur Basso continuo

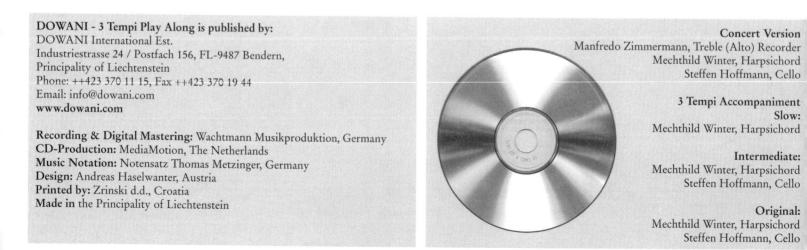

DOWANI - 3 Tempi Play Along is published by:
DOWANI International Est.
Industriestrasse 24 / Postfach 156, FL-9487 Bendern,
Principality of Liechtenstein
Phone: ++423 370 11 15, Fax ++423 370 19 44
Email: info@dowani.com
www.dowani.com

Recording & Digital Mastering: Wachtmann Musikproduktion, Germany
CD-Production: MediaMotion, The Netherlands
Music Notation: Notensatz Thomas Metzinger, Germany
Design: Andreas Haselwanter, Austria
Printed by: Zrinski d.d., Croatia
Made in the Principality of Liechtenstein

Concert Version
Manfredo Zimmermann, Treble (Alto) Recorder
Mechthild Winter, Harpsichord
Steffen Hoffmann, Cello

3 Tempi Accompaniment
Slow:
Mechthild Winter, Harpsichord

Intermediate:
Mechthild Winter, Harpsichord
Steffen Hoffmann, Cello

Original:
Mechthild Winter, Harpsichord
Steffen Hoffmann, Cello